IDOLS OF POP

BILLIE EILISH

YOUR **UNOFFICIAL** GUIDE TO THE MOST TALKED ABOUT TEEN ON THE PLANET

IDOLS OF POP

BILLIE EILISH

YOUR UNOFFICIAL GUIDE TO THE MOST TALKED ABOUT TEEN ON THE PLANET

Amy Wills

HARPER

An Imprint of HarperCollinsPublishers

Billie
cleans up at the
2020
Grammys

CONTENTS

WHO IS BILLIE EILISH? 6

THE EARLY YEARS 8

A STAR IS BORN 10

6 REASONS WE LOVE BILLIE 12

BILLIE BY NUMBERS 14

SHE'S IN FASHION 16

BEAUTY SECRETS 18

6 FACTS ABOUT BILLIE 20

BILLIE'S HAIR 22

WHEN WE ALL FALL ASLEEP, WHERE DO WE GO? 24

THE WORLD ACCORDING TO BILLIE 26

BILLIE ON TOUR 28

BEST MUSIC VIDEOS 30

BILLIE VS. FAME 32

WHO IS FINNEAS? 34

BILLIE'S FAVORITE THINGS 36

THE ULTIMATE BILLIE PLAYLIST 38

BILLIE OPENS UP 40

VOICE OF A GENERATION 42

SCREEN IDOL 44

BILLIE'S INFLUENCES 46

BILLIE EXPLAINS IT ALL 48

TIMES BILLIE EILISH WAS ALL OF US 50

BILLIE VS. SOCIAL MEDIA 52

FAMOUS FANS 54

BILLIE ON LOVE 56

THINGS BILLIE HATES 58

ALBUM NUMBER TWO 60

BILLIE ♥ HER FANS 62

WHO IS BILLIE EILISH?

How one teenage pop star is reinventing the music industry

In October 2015, 13-year-old Billie Eilish uploaded her first song, **"Ocean Eyes,"** to SoundCloud late one night in her LA bedroom. She had only intended for one person to listen to it: her dance teacher. When she woke up the next day, the song had **gone viral** around the world, with over 1,000 listens (it's now had almost **40 million**).

Her music defies genre—it's been called pop, EDM, industrial, trap, and even jazz—her voice ranges from a muted whisper to a belted-out chorus, and her strange lyrics blend point of view and gender roles. **Speaking specifically to the anxieties of Gen Z** (her album addresses climate change, teen suicide, and sobriety) and also dealing with timeless themes like love and death, Billie Eilish has fans of every age.

From her first song, things skyrocketed. Billie Eilish (pronounced eye-lish) signed a record deal with Darkroom/Interscope Records. Her first single, **"bad guy,"** went straight to the top of the charts, making her the first artist born this century to have a US number 1.

She released her first album, ***When We All Fall Asleep, Where Do We Go?***, in 2019 to universal critical acclaim and record-breaking chart domination.

With her own distinctive punk style, "neo-goth" aesthetic, and irreverent social media voice, she challenges expectations of what a female pop star can sound like, look like, and publicly say.

She's played **Coachella**, **Glastonbury**, and performed at the **Oscars**. She's the youngest ever artist to record the **Bond theme tune**. At the **2020 Grammys**, Billie Eilish made history as the second artist in the show's history to win all four major categories: **Best New Artist**, **Record of the Year**, **Album of the Year**, and **Song of the Year**. At 18, she's the **youngest Grammy winner to win all four nominations** on the same night and the first woman to do so.

THE EARLY YEARS

Although it feels like she came out of nowhere and took over the world, Billie has a backstory . . .

Billie Eilish Pirate Baird O'Connell was born in **2001** in the **Highland Park** area of **Los Angeles**. This now popular place was not always so appealing. Billie describes it as being *"really sketchy"* during her childhood.

Billie was also homeschooled, and her mom taught her a beginner's songwriting course. *"When I see movies set in summertime, that's what my life was like all the time, but it doesn't mean I didn't learn,"* says Billie. *"My mom would cook and she'd be like, 'How much goes into this?' And that's how we learned."*

She lived with her *"built-in best friend"* and older brother, **Finneas** (more on him later), and her parents, **Maggie Baird** and **Patrick O'Connell**, who were working actors. They were raised vegetarian and slept in a four-person family bed until Finneas was 10.

Little Billie loved dancing, horse riding, and singing in the Los Angeles Children's Chorus. She was also a budding fashion designer, building costumes and making accessories from scratch.

Her dream was to be a dancer, until injuries meant she had to give it up. But dancing's loss was music's gain. *"I've always known that singing, writing music, and performing is what I've wanted to do,"* she says. We are glad it worked out, Billie!

A STAR IS BORN

From making music in her bedroom to making history

"**Ocean Eyes**" was just the beginning. Although she was only 14, Billie signed a record deal with Interscope and, instead of just bringing out "Ocean Eyes" as a single, she got to work on her EP. In the summer of 2017 she released *Don't Smile at Me*. "My EP is called Don't Smile at Me *for a lot of reasons, but one of them would be when [someone tells you],* 'Smile. Why aren't you smiling? It's so much more beautiful when you smile.'"

Billie finally dropped her long-awaited and first full-length album on March 29, 2019. Billie was nervous just before **When We All Fall Asleep, Where Do We Go?** dropped, afraid people wouldn't love it like she did. *"I didn't want the world to be able to tell me how they feel about this thing I love,"* she confesses. *"But the response has been crazy."* It went straight to the **top of the chart** in the **UK** and the **US**.

Two weeks later she began her album tour with a coveted slot at the music festival **Coachella**. She went on to win a clutch of awards, break records, be named Billboard's Woman of the Year, and record the song for the **James Bond** movie *No Time to Die*. And she's still only 18. **Wow!**

6 REASONS WE LOVE BILLIE

Um, 'cause she's the best . . .

1 SHE KEEPS IT REAL

We can't think of many pop stars who would begin their debut album with the words "I've taken out my Invisalign and this is my album" but that's how Billie's kicks off. What a legend.

2 SHE'S POLITICAL

Billie has used her platform to speak out about everything from gun control to climate change. She recently took part in a campaign encouraging people to register to vote. Billie for president!

3 SHE'S A TRUE ORIGINAL

Billie has no interest in blending into the crowd. *"I've always known what I want and who I wanted to be, what I wanted to wear and who I wanted to be seen as."* You do you, Billie.

4 SHE CALLS OUT INJUSTICE

When *Nylon* magazine mocked up a strange cover of a topless, hairless Billie, she wasn't going to take it lying down. She called them out as having done it without her consent in a totally justified response to a very uncool use of her image.

5 SHE JUST DOESN'T CARE

Whether she's wearing a head-to-toe baggy jumpsuit or dyeing her hair bright green, Billie has confidence. *"I like to dress memorable,"* she says. *"I love being in people's heads, so if you are thinking about me, but what you're thinking about is like 'Oh, she looks so bad' or 'That's so ugly,' I don't even care!"* We will remember this next time someone gives us *the look.*

6 SHE'S MADE POP COOL AGAIN

With so much talk about the music industry dying, Billie has resurrected it. She's made it cool to like pop. Billie, we salute you!

BILLIE BY NUMBERS

What's the secret to Billie's success? Let's figure it out

2.36 BILLION
The number of streams *When We All Fall Asleep, Where Do We Go?* had in 2019

5
The number of Grammy awards Billie has

60+ MILLION
The number of followers Billie has on Instagram

$8 MILLION
Her estimated worth

29+ MILLION
The number of Billie's subscribers on YouTube

12
The age she was when she fell for her "first love," Justin Bieber

833 MILLION

Views for "bad guy," her most-watched video on YouTube

800

Billie jokes her clothes are this many sizes too big for her

10,000

hours is written on Finneas's wall to remind him of how much dedication is needed

13

The number of different hair colors Billie's had

13

The age she was when she recorded the vocals for "Ocean Eyes"

5' 3"

How tall Billie is

2014

The year Billie went vegan

007

Billie is the youngest artist to record a Bond theme tune

8

The track on her album where she plays ukulele (it was originally called 7)

SHE'S IN FASHION

Billie's wardrobe is as distinctive as her music

From highlighter hair to oversize clothes, face masks to high-vis vests, Billie's fashion sense is like no one else's. *"I always wanted to wear whatever I wanted to wear. No one has ever told me otherwise even when I was a kid. Clothing is my safety net, it's like my security guard."*

FEBRUARY 2019
Road safety, but make it fashion

In May 2019, in an ad for Calvin Klein, Billie shared with the world the reason she always wears baggy clothing. *"I never want the world to know everything about me,"* she says. *"That's why I wear big, baggy clothes. Nobody can have an opinion because they haven't seen what's underneath."*

SEPTEMBER 2018
Oversize, neon colors, totally rad
—this look is 100% Billie

She's also calling out the sexism in the music industry. *"If I was a guy and I was wearing these baggy clothes, nobody would bat an eye. There's people out there saying, 'Dress like a girl for once! Wear tight clothes, you'd be much prettier and your career would be so much better!' No it wouldn't."* Girl power.

NOVEMBER 2019
Rocking head-to-toe Burberry and a full-face veil

NOVEMBER 2019
Who knew satin Gucci pajamas, sneakers, and two-tone green hair could look so good?

Cementing her status as a fashion icon, Billie recently designed fashion collections with Urban Outfitters, Bershka, and H&M. *"I really like fashion, I'm already doing a lot with it because it is just part of who I am. I feel like I might be a designer or stylist."* Watch this space.

BEAUTY SECRETS

We've collected all Billie's best tips so you don't have to rummage through her makeup bag!

Brow Power

Billie is known for her trademark full, bushy eyebrows. Her makeup artist, Robert Rumsey, uses a brow pencil to "draw the hairs in the direction of the natural growth. It's more modern than filling in the entire brow." Then he adds a clear brow gel to set the look.

The Billie basics

"Don't touch your face! I always make it a habit not to. I wash my face every night and apply a moisturizer or else my skin will flake off into a million pieces. Essentially, I always make sure to drink a lot of water, sleep, and not touch my face."

Less is more

When it comes to her skin, Billie likes to keep it natural. "You don't need a ton of products," says Robert. "A good foundation and concealer. I prefer buildable products. I like translucent loose powder for the T-zone and cream highlighters that aren't sticky."

Got it nailed

Billie has started wearing long acrylic green nails, even wearing customized Gucci ones to the Grammys. But she often shares pictures on Instagram of broken nails.

Get rid of the gloss

Robert says he avoids two products when Billie performs on stage: lip gloss and sticky highlighter. "Billie has long hair and I don't want it sticking to her face," he told Yahoo.

Go for glow

"My inspo for the AMAs was glow, glow, GLOW," says Robert. "I knew she was performing with fire around her. I kept the skin clean with flawless, bushy brows, and perfectly separated lashes. Always a wet lip."

And if all else fails . . .

Wear a mask and sunglasses. Duh.

6 FACTS ABOUT BILLIE

A few things you might not know about being Billie

1 SHE HAS SYNESTHESIA

Billie has synesthesia, a condition in which senses seem to blend together because of neurosensory wire-crossing. It means objects such as words or numbers can be joined with a sensory perception such as smell, flavor, or color. According to Billie, her song "bad guy" is red, yellow, and the number seven.

2 SHE IS LACTOSE-INTOLERANT

Billie grew up vegetarian and officially switched to a vegan lifestyle in 2014. Regarding her choice, she went to Tumblr to explain why she decided to go free of animal products in her diet. In 2018, she wrote on her blog, "*I went vegan like four years ago. There were a lot of reasons. I love animals and also I'm lactose intolerant.*"

5 SHE HAS TOURETTE'S

In 2018, the singer confirmed that she had Tourette's syndrome, a condition that causes a person to have involuntary tics. She specifically experiences physical tics as opposed to verbal ones. "*I've taught myself ways of suppressing my tics and certain techniques to help reduce them when I don't want to be distracting in certain situations,*" she explained in an Instagram story.

3 SHE LOVES HORSES

Billie worked in barns to afford riding lessons. She recently collaborated with Urban Outfitters to donate money to Red Bucket Equine Rescue, an organization that rehabilitates and rescues horses.

6 SHE'S A MOVIE STAR (KIND OF)

As a child she recorded background vocals for films such as *Diary of a Wimpy Kid* and the X-Men series.

4 SHE'S A HORROR MOVIE FAN

Her favorite movie is *The Babadook*.

BILLIE'S HAIR

Blue? Green? Black? Silver? Billie has had some serious transformations in the hair department

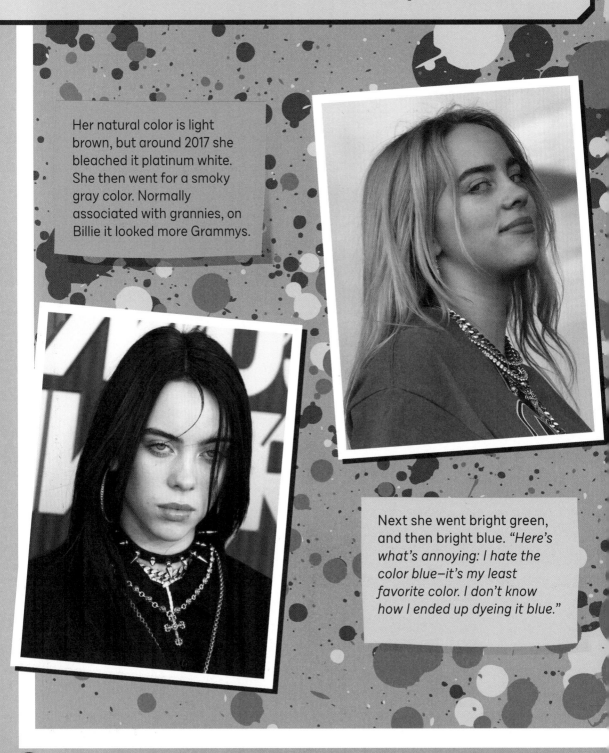

Her natural color is light brown, but around 2017 she bleached it platinum white. She then went for a smoky gray color. Normally associated with grannies, on Billie it looked more Grammys.

Next she went bright green, and then bright blue. *"Here's what's annoying: I hate the color blue—it's my least favorite color. I don't know how I ended up dyeing it blue."*

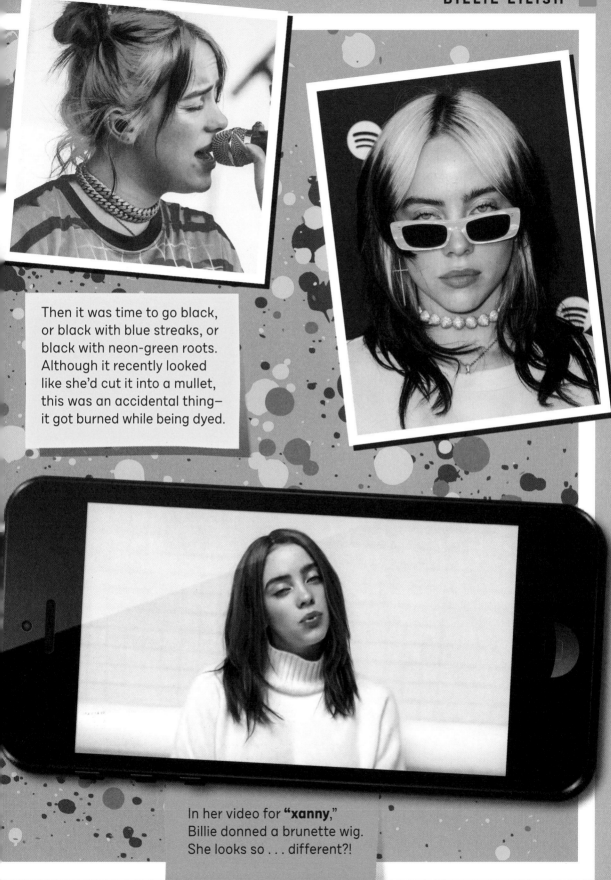

Then it was time to go black, or black with blue streaks, or black with neon-green roots. Although it recently looked like she'd cut it into a mullet, this was an accidental thing— it got burned while being dyed.

In her video for **"xanny,"** Billie donned a brunette wig. She looks so . . . different?!

WHEN WE ALL FALL ASLEEP, WHERE DO WE GO?

A complete track-by-track breakdown

THE BEGINNING

The album's opening track, **"!!!!!!!,"** is just Billie slurping saliva, announcing *"this is the album,"* and descending into laughter. Then it's straight into pop-trap song **"bad guy,"** which uses a bass, a kick drum, and finger clicks. Then there's **"xanny."** While recording this song, Billie and her brother created a sound inspired by a girl blowing cigarette smoke in someone's face alongside a drum kit and a jazz-inspired loop. So now we know what that sounds like.

THE MIDDLE

"you should see me in a crown" is all blaring synths and electropop. Then **"all the good girls go to hell"** is a punchy piano number. **"wish you were gay"** is a jazzy pop song, and **"when the party's over"** was written after Finneas had left his date's house for *"kind of no reason."* We've all been there.

THE COVER

The shoot for the cover art took place on Billie's 17th birthday at a studio in LA and lasted twelve hours. Billie had prepared sketches for the album cover inspired by night terrors and lucid dreaming, and horror movies such as *The Babadook*. Photographer Kenneth Cappello added no additional lighting to the end photo so as to give the impression that *"a door was opening and that was the light coming into the bedroom."* Billie wore contact lenses to fill in her eyes completely with white.

MORE MIDDLE

"8"–appropriately enough the eighth track on the album–is a ukulele-based lullaby. So it's quite a shift to **"my strange addiction,"** a bass-heavy pop banger that samples *The Office*. **"bury a friend"** is a minimalist electronica with synth melodies. The beat leads seamlessly into **"ilomilo,"** named after the video game.

THE END

The final three tracks each talk about saying farewell, collectively reading **"listen before i go,"** **"i love you,"** and **"goodbye."** "goodbye" features a line of each of the album's tracks (with the exception of "!!!!!!!") in its lyrics in reverse order compared with how they appear in the album, beginning with a line from "i love you" and ending with a line from "bad guy," with clips from these songs layered quietly in reverse.

THE WORLD ACCORDING TO BILLIE

Say it, girl

"In the public eye, girls and women with strong perspectives are hated. If you're a girl with an opinion, people just hate you. That's so lame."

We are printing this out and sticking it on our bedroom wall.

"I've always done whatever I want and always been exactly who I am."

"There are always going to be bad things. But you can write it down and make a song out of it."

"I'm not going to say I'm cool. I just don't care at all, and I guess that's what people think is cool."

Aww.

"I feel like I write so that people can think of it as theirs. If my song is exactly about your life right now, then it is."

BILLIE ON TOUR

Never made it to a Billie Eilish concert? This is almost as good as seeing her live

COACHELLA

This was a big moment for Billie; she was one of the most talked-about performers at the festival. The crowd went crazy, and knew all the words to her songs, even if Billie didn't. While singing **"all the good girls go to hell,"** Billie forgot the lyrics. To be fair, the album had only come out a few weeks before.

When she plays the song "COPYCAT," it often starts a mosh pit.

She uses creepy props.

When a fan threw underwear onstage and it hit her, she said *"OK, that's the energy, I get it."*

ONE BY ONE TOUR, DENMARK

Are you even a pop star until you've fallen over onstage? Billie was singing **"bury a friend"** when she slipped on the floor. She lay on the floor for a few minutes and carried on singing from there. **What a pro.**

RADIO 1 LIVE LOUNGE

Billie did a cover of Phantogram's **"You Don't Get Me High Anymore"** while wearing a skeleton hoodie. *"I might bomb it,"* she said before she started, but of course she nailed it.

THE GREEK THEATRE, LA

For a stripped-back acoustic performance of **"i love you,"** Billie and her brother, Finneas, performed on a floating bed, because they wrote the song on her bed at two in the morning. Billie dedicated the song to a friend who had passed away and it was so poignant, many people there were reduced to tears, including Billie.

BAD GUY ON SNL

So what if she's got a sprained ankle? For this Halloween performance Billie Eilish literally climbed up the walls and danced on the ceiling. *Cooool.*

She often arrives onstage to music from a Nintendo Wii.

BEST MUSIC VIDEOS

From the creepy to the, uh, creepier, these are our favorite Billie videos

7 **bury a friend**

Like a mini horror movie, this video has Billie play a black-eyed monster hiding under the bed. She's then injected with needles, levitates in hallways, gets grabbed by disembodied hands, and then watches someone sleep. Shivers.

6 **you should see me in a crown**

Billie teamed up with artist and animator Takashi Murakami for this video, which features a cartoon Billie. It's cute until Billie transforms into a monster-size spider with a human skull face who destroys a city.

5 **idontwannabeyouanymore**

Sometimes it's the simple things that can be the most effective, like this video! It is just Billie dressed in a white boiler suit, in a white room, looking at herself in the mirror. Weirdly, it's captivating.

4 when the party's over

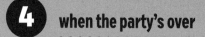

The shots of Billie crying thick black ink in this video were inspired by a drawing she received from a fan. Billie actually had tubes on her face that spurted out the charcoal and gum solution into her eyes.

3 xanny

Billie made her directorial debut with the video for this song. She looks normcore, with a brunette wig on a cream bench. And then hands enter and put cigarettes out on her face. Ouch!

2 everything i wanted

Also directed by Billie, this video is dedicated to Finneas and shows Billie and her brother going for a drive through LA. Then they drive into the ocean. The car fills with water and everything goes black.

1 bad guy

Bloody nose? Two heads in plastic bags? Pouring milk in someone's mouth? Sitting on someone's back while they do push-ups? No, it's not a fever dream, it's the video for "bad guy," of course!

BILLIE Vs. FAME

Think being a mega-famous pop star is all it's cracked up to be? Think again

It's a love / hate thing

Considering she found fame virtually overnight, it's not surprising Billie Eilish feels a bit ambivalent about it. *"I hate it. But it's great, though. I don't mean that to sound ungrateful. It's a really hard thing and hurts, but who cares?"* Mixed feelings then, we guess.

OK, sometimes it's just a hate thing

Billie doesn't want to dislike fame, but she's good at admitting that some parts are a drag. *"I have this amazing thing in front of me, and I don't want to hate it. And I don't hate it. But I hate certain parts of it."*

Household name

She now has the kind of notoriety where people stop her on the street. *"It's like nothing I would ever think it is,"* she says. *"When this kind of thing happens, you just have to be like, 'let's just go with it.'"*

The good old days

But it wasn't always like this. *"For a minute, I could go somewhere nobody knew who I was,"* she says. *"I would go places and try to convince myself I wasn't famous or whatever."*

It's lonely at the top

If you're one of Billie's friends, it can be hard to understand her fame. *"I've definitely lost a lot of people. When I hang out with people I haven't seen in a while, I say the things that are going on in my life and people think I'm bragging. I'm not bragging, I'm just telling you about my life."*

She won't let it go to her head

So don't expect her to start acting like a diva. *"What I know is that I never want to feel famous in my head. I've already seen how gross it can make you."*

But she likes it really . . .

"I like being famous. It's very weird, but it's very cool."

WHO IS FINNEAS?

He's waaaay more than just Billie's brother, that's for sure

If you're a Billie fan, you'll already know all about her big bro, Finneas, who cowrites and produces all her songs. So what else do we know about him?

Finneas O'Connell was born on July 20, 1997, which makes him five years older than Billie.

If you recognize him, it might be because he played Alistair in the TV show *Glee* and also appeared in *Modern Family*.

Finneas is the lead singer of The Slightlys. That's actually who he wrote the song "Ocean Eyes" for originally.

He's been dating YouTuber Claudia Sulewski since 2018, and even wrote a song called "Claudia" about her, which he wrote after the first night they met. *Aww.*

Along with writing songs for Billie, he's also written songs for YouTube singer Rebecca Black.

"We're a pretty close-knit family to begin with so that's not really super new," says Finneas about touring with Billie. *"We get along really well so it's been really nice."*

"Me and Finneas have always had a bond," Billie reveals. *"We've always had a connection, especially with music."*

BILLIE'S FAVORITE THINGS

We're all fans of Billie's, but what is she a fan of?

THE OFFICE

Billie is a big fan of the **Steve Carell** show. So much so that she even sampled a song from the episode called **"Threat Level Midnight."** *"When we made the beat for "***my strange addiction***," it reminded me of the song they play when they do the Scarn dance. Also, it's about strange addictions, and* **The Office** *is mine, so . . ."*

JUSTIN BIEBER

Billie has made no secret about being a Belieber. *"It wasn't like I was just a fan, man. I've been in love before, and it was with him,"* she told *Marie Claire*. She finally got to meet him at Coachella, and the pair collaborated on a remix of **"bad guy"** so now they're totally friends.

AVOCADOS

And it's not just because she has green hair. Her Instagram handle used to be **WhereAreTheAvocados**. And here is why. *"Six years ago, I wanna say, I was in my house, home alone, making a grilled cheese,"* Billie says. *"I was almost done, you know, I was getting everything ready and I wanted some avocados, so I opened the fridge and was like, 'Where are the avocados?' And in my head I was like, that'd be funny if I made that my username."* So now we know.

ANIMALS

A vegan since 2014 and an enthusiastic horse-rider, Billie is a friend to furry creatures. *"Horses are the most therapeutic animals. And cows, dude. People eat those—that's crazy."* We'll never look at a burger in the same way again.

THE MOSH PIT

You know that scary part at the front of a gig where everyone is diving around going crazy? Billie loves it. *"I love movement. I love moshing. I always head right for the front and dig in there and mosh really hard with all the guys."*

THE ULTIMATE BILLIE PLAYLIST

There's a Billie tune for every mood

You're feeling whimsical . . . ?
Play . . . **party favor**

This sweet-sounding tune from her debut EP, *Don't Smile at Me,* is a twinkly, plinky soundscape about breaking up with someone on their birthday. This is as cute and catchy as Billie gets.

You're feeling shy . . . ?
Play . . . **come out and play**

Billie and Finneas wrote this song for the Apple Christmas ad and it's all about not hiding away and making your mark on the world. "You don't have to keep it quiet / I know it makes you nervous / but I promise you it's worth it."

You're feeling fired up . . . ?
Play . . . &burn

In this collaboration with rapper Vince Staples, Billie delivers a sassy, attitude-laden tune about watching someone's car burn, and her heart burn. Basically, this song is on fire!

You're feeling sassy . . . ?
Play . . . COPYCAT

"Call me cocky, watch your tone / You better love me, 'cause you're just a clone," Billie commands on the opening track of her debut EP, *Don't Smile at Me*. This song makes fans go crazy when Billie performs it live. "Psych!"

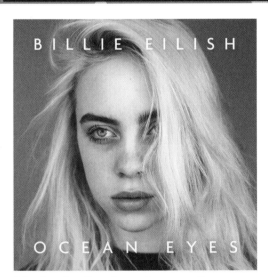

You're feeling loved-up . . . ?
Play . . . Ocean Eyes

From its opening whispers to its crooning chorus, Billie's breakthrough single is all about watching someone from afar, falling into their eyes, and compares falling in love to falling off a cliff under "napalm skies."

You're feeling creepy . . . ?
Play . . . bellyache

Despite starting off as a twee slice of folk-pop, this gets dark. Billie adopts the mindset of a teenage serial killer slaughtering her nearest and dearest. Don't try this at home.

BILLIE OPENS UP

She's not afraid to tackle the big issues and say what's on her mind

DARK TIMES

Billie has been open about her battles with her mental health, helping millions of fans who also feel this way. *"Depression has controlled sort of everything in my life . . . I've kind of always been a melancholy person,"* she admitted to **Zane Lowe** on **Beats 1**. But she's used her struggles with her mood to help her fans. *"I just grab my fans by the shoulders and I'm like, 'Please take care of yourself and be good to yourself and be nice to yourself.'"*

CLIMATE CHANGE

We're all worried about global warming, and Billie has been very vocal about her fears that we're not doing enough to stop it. *"It's weird . . . It feels like we're living in a movie that you'd watch where the world is like ending. I want to have children and I want them to have children."* At the **American Music Awards**, Billie wore a T-shirt showing her support for **Music Declares Emergency**, an activist group of artists and music professionals. Their mission to acknowledge the environmental impact of the music industry struck a chord with Billie, who has partnered with a nonprofit company to keep her tour as green as possible.

BODY ISSUES

Wearing baggy clothes has now become Billie's signature style. But she recently revealed that the reason it came about was because puberty made her uncomfortable about her body. *"I just hated my body,"* she says. *"I would have done anything to be in a different one."* Thankfully Billie always wears what she wants to wear despite the criticisms, and is very vocal about women in the industry not being judged by superficial standards.

VOICE OF A GENERATION

There's never been a pop star like Billie before. Here's how she encapsulates the zeitgeist . . .

SHE'S HONEST

Billie is incredibly candid about what's really on her mind. She's open about the downsides of fame and isn't afraid to be vulnerable about her mental health issues and her Tourette's.

SHE OPTS OUT OF WEARING REVEALING CLOTHES

Billie's style rejects traditional ways of dressing according to gender—for example, girls wearing super tight clothes. Her stylist, **Samantha Burkhart**, says Billie *"is not buying into the hypersexualized idea of what femininity is."*

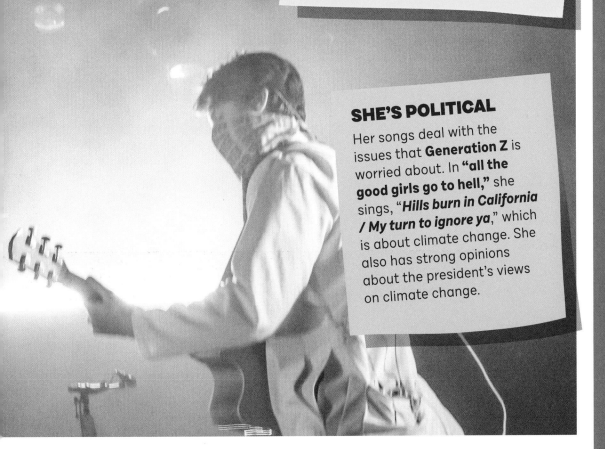

SHE'S POLITICAL

Her songs deal with the issues that **Generation Z** is worried about. In **"all the good girls go to hell,"** she sings, *"Hills burn in California / My turn to ignore ya,"* which is about climate change. She also has strong opinions about the president's views on climate change.

SCREEN IDOL

Billie's music on the big screen

13 REASONS WHY WE LOVE BILLIE

Billie has had two songs appear on the soundtracks to the Netflix series *13 Reasons Why*. **"Bored"** appeared during season one, and **"lovely"** was on season two, right when Clay talks with Hannah for the last time before the funeral and finishes his semicolon tattoo.

ROMA

Billie also released a typically moody ballad—**"WHEN I WAS OLDER"**—for an album of songs inspired by **Alfonso Cuarón's** 2018 movie *Roma*. The song is inspired by something said by Pepe, a character in *Roma*: *"When I was older I used to be a sailor, but I drowned in a storm."* Billie and Finneas fell so in love with the film, which also won Best Foreign Language Film at the Oscars and the Golden Globes, that they got to work on a new track.

THE NAME'S EILISH, BILLIE EILISH

In January 2020, it was confirmed that Billie was following in the footsteps of Adele and Sam Smith by recording the theme music to the **James Bond** movie *No Time to Die*.
Billie and Finneas have always been big fans of the franchise, and writing the theme song is a dream come true. *"James Bond is the coolest film franchise ever to exist. I'm still in shock,"* Billie says.

BILLIE'S INFLUENCES

She has made a sound all her own, but here's what inspires Billie

OTHER MUSICIANS

From rap to Lana Del Rey, the music on Billie's stereo has shaped her. *"Tyler, the Creator has probably been, overall, the biggest influence musically. I'm also really inspired by a lot of rappers because a lot of the stuff that real rappers say is kind of ahead of what other people are saying—artists like Tyler, Earl Sweatshirt, Odd Future, and Brockhampton. Of course, I also love Lana Del Rey and Amy Winehouse. I could name a million."*

THE WALKING DEAD

Billie's first foray into songwriting was inspired by the zombie TV show *The Walking Dead*. Her first ever song was about the zombie apocalypse. It's called *"Fingers Crossed."* Billie says, *"I literally just watched* The Walking Dead *and I took little lines from it. Just watch it and you'll find some things that are in my song and some episode titles that are in my song."*

NATURE

Like being in green spaces? So does Billie. She loves to take her ukulele up to the tree house built by her dad. So cool.

THE NEIGHBOURHOOD

Watching this band in LA was Billie's first gig and she says *Wiped Out!* by **The Neighbourhood** is the soundtrack to her life. "It touches on a lot of different emotions at once—I think that is a good description of how my year has been. Surreal and kind of really cool, but a lot of bad things also happened, so it is kind of a mix of everything."

HER MOM

Billie's mom, Maggie, goes everywhere with her and was one of her earliest role models. "She's been with me through all of this and [has been] taking me at my horrible self. She taught me how to write music . . . I could go on about her." Aww.

BILLIE EXPLAINS IT ALL

What's really going on in Billie's lyrics?

"She's a serial killer!"

"She's a monster!"

Billie is certainly no one-trick pony when it comes to songwriting. She composes songs about anything and everything, which is why people of all ages and from all walks of life relate so strongly to her. Let's look at a few of her songs and what they're all about:

BAD GUY

Billie's iconic song makes fun of everyone who pretends to be something they are not. We all now know that if we call ourselves bad guys or rule breakers, we're probably not . . .

BURY A FRIEND

In this song, Billie reminds us of the importance of thinking about and doing things for yourself rather than giving all of yourself, including your love, to someone or something else and losing yourself in the process.

IDONTWANNABEYOUANYMORE

This song is about the way Billie feels about herself and her battles with depression. She wishes she had more confidence and was more secure in her abilities. She gets really honest about how, at times in her life, she has felt sad every day, and how she sometimes doesn't want to be herself.

BELLYACHE

In this one, Billie sings about a fictional psychopath who kills off their friends. They regret being a psychopath but don't really care. Ummm, not sure we can relate to this one.

TIMES BILLIE EILISH WAS ALL OF US

She might be a superstar, but so many things about Billie have us shouting, "Same!"

SHE LOVES FREE STUFF

We all love free stuff and Billie now gets sent everything from jewelry to fake nails, but she's most excited about Nikes: *"All I wanted was a pair of Nikes, and I couldn't afford them. And now I have hundreds in my house. Unreal."*

SHE'S STRUGGLED TO FIT IN

We've all had our moments of trying to fit in and be just like everyone else. And while Billie is very much her own person these days, even she also went through an uncertain phase when she was younger: *"I tried to fit in . . . It was the worst year ever."*

SHE'S RELATABLE

Take this tweet, for example. *"i just smiled at a manikin thinking it was a person"*. We've all been there.

SHE GETS DOWN

Billie has been very open about her mental health issues, but also what she does to manage them. *"It doesn't make you weak to ask for help. And you should be able to ask anyone for help, everyone has to help someone if they need it."*

SHE STILL LIVES AT HOME

In a two-bedroom bungalow with her mom, dad, a rescue cat, **Misha**, a rescue dog, **Pepper**, and her spider. *"I'm lucky to have a family that I like, and that likes me,"* she says. And she still has to clean her own room.

BILLIE VS. SOCIAL MEDIA

It's not all likes, y'know

YOUTUBE

Billie has called out YouTubers who've dressed up like her to make prank videos. She asked people to *"please stop. It is not safe for you and it is mean to the people who don't know any better . . . you make me look bad."*

TWITTER

She has 4.1 million followers on Twitter, but after going through a dark time when she was in Europe, she no longer handles her own Twitter account. Good for Billie for distancing herself from all the opinions.

INSTAGRAM

She is on Insta and her username used to be the enigmatic **@wherearetheavocados**. She's now **@billieeilish**. The first picture she ever posted was of her thumb. She says her favorite Instagram accounts are stylists and fashion designers such as **Bloody Osiris**, **Imran Potato**, and sneaker addict **Lil Jupiter**.

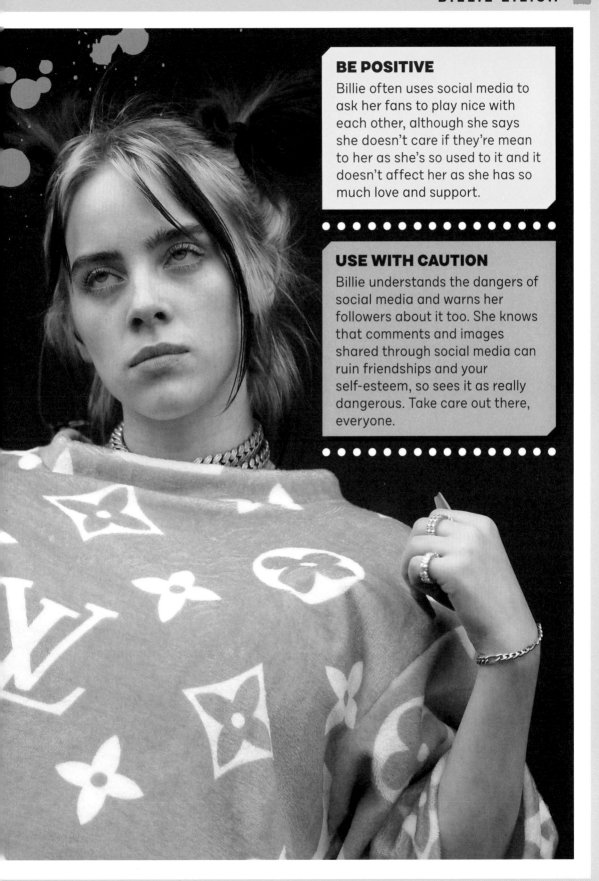

BE POSITIVE

Billie often uses social media to ask her fans to play nice with each other, although she says she doesn't care if they're mean to her as she's so used to it and it doesn't affect her as she has so much love and support.

USE WITH CAUTION

Billie understands the dangers of social media and warns her followers about it too. She knows that comments and images shared through social media can ruin friendships and your self-esteem, so sees it as really dangerous. Take care out there, everyone.

FAMOUS FANS

Billie's most A-list superfans, ranked

1

ELTON JOHN

Legendary star, songwriter, and musician Elton John loves Billie and thinks she's a unique new talent. He can't wait to see her live. You know you've made it when Elton John's at your show!

2

LANA DEL REY

Billie and Lana Del Rey have a special musical connection, as Billie cited Lana as one of her biggest influences. And the singer-songwriter loves Billie right back! Us too, Lana. Us too.

3

DAVE GROHL

The **Foo Fighters** frontman has said that his daughters are obsessed with Billie and he's likened the connection she has with her audience to the fans Nirvana had in the 1990s.

4

KATY PERRY

There were "fireworks" when Katy met Billie at the legendary **Coachella Festival**. Katy even posted on Instagram celebrating Billie as a unique and rare new talent in the industry!

5

SHAWN MENDES

The "**Señorita**" singer gave Billie a big up on Twitter, telling his fans how talented she is. Billie also revealed in an interview that Shawn had texted her but she hadn't replied. Whoops!

6

NIALL HORAN

Billie has fans all over the world and pop royalty is no exception, which was clear when 1D's Niall Horan tweeted out that he was bopping along to Billie's awesome album.

7

DEMI LOVATO

Girl power! Pop princess Demi Lovato is a massive Billie fan, taking the time to listen to Billie's awesome music and sharing her love and admiration with her fans on Instagram.

8

THOM YORKE

Iconically weird and wonderful Radiohead front man Thom Yorke is a big fan of the way Billie follows her own path and does her own thing. She's her own person, just like Thom!

BILLIE ON LOVE

Although she's very private about her love life, this is what we know about Billie's heart

SHE'S A FAN OF SELF LOVE

"*I'm in love with myself . . . I'm in love with her,*" she said, gesturing to herself. Something we should all be emulating!

HER FIRST KISS WAS A DISAPPOINTMENT

Billie dished about her unfortunate experience at a concert in March 2018. "*Two years ago, I went to the movies with a boy,*" she recalls. "*Right after we kissed, he says, 'Wow, that was really not as magical at all as I thought it was going to be,'*" she shares. Ouch.

SHE DOESN'T WANT HER FANS TO LOVE HER

After her own experience with being a superfan of Justin Bieber, Billie is suprised at how her fans feel the same way about her. "*I do not mean to be putting anybody in the position I was in. That hurts.*"

HER FIRST LOVE WAS JUSTIN BIEBER

"*I can't even explain it to sound normal–I was in love with him. It was so miserable. It's not a good feeling to be in love with someone who doesn't know you exist.*" We get it– Justin Bieber = swoon!

THINGS BILLIE HATES

Haters gonna hate, but here are all the things that Billie dislikes

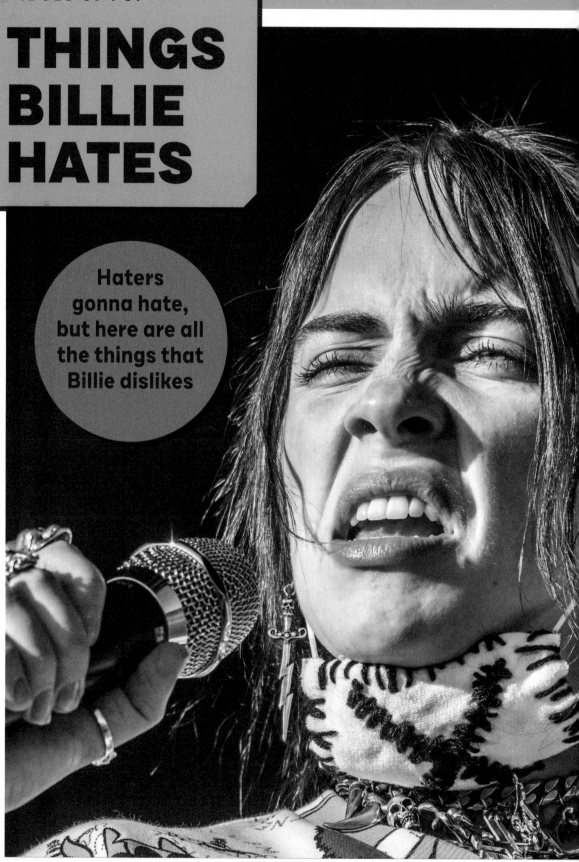

SMILING

Don't expect to see many pictures of Billie flashing a cheesy grin. She hates smiling and can often be seen with what she describes as *"resting brat face."* We will totally channel this when someone tells us to cheer up.

GETTING OLD

Billie doesn't ever want to be as old as, uh, 27! We're not sure there's much you can do about that one.

FANS COMING TO HER HOUSE

When the singer's address was leaked online, overly enthusiastic fans began showing up at Billie's childhood home, which understandably left her shaken.

NIGHTMARES

Her album might be called *When We All Fall Asleep, Where Do We Go?* but Billie doesn't go somewhere dreamy when she tucks in at night. She regularly experiences **night terrors** and **nightmares**.

DRUGS

Billie has never done any drugs and is quite outspoken about it. She wrote the song **"xanny"** about her experiences of watching her friends drink at a party. Great attitude, Billie!

ALBUM NUMBER 2

Here's everything we know so far about Billie's second album

WILL THERE BE ANY COLLABORATIONS ON THE SECOND ALBUM?

Yes! Back in March, Spanish singer **Rosalía** tweeted a photo of her and Billie, captioning it with *"Can't wait to finish our song."* The singer was mightily impressed with Billie's work ethic and passion, and by all accounts these two had a great time in the studio together. We're not jealous at all . . . **Tyler, the Creator** has also said he wants to team up. Billie is a big fan of the rapper and we think this collaboration would be a-maz-ing!

WHEN WE ALL FALL ASLEEP

WHEN IS IT COMING OUT?

Although rumors swirled during summer 2019 that she was about to drop another album, Billie was quick to shoot them down. So don't hold your breath for a 2020 release. But don't worry, she's assured fans it's coming.

HOW FAR THROUGH MAKING IT IS SHE?

Finneas explains to fans that they're deep in the creative process working on the new material. He also indicated that they're making music while touring, which is easier without all the usual distractions at home.

SHE'S WATCHING US

Before each show, Billie is driven around the venue to look through the windows at the fans waiting outside. Aww!

SHE THINKS WE LOOK SICK

Billie appreciates our style. Before her shows, Billie likes to check out what her fans are wearing. *"They always look really cool."* Thanks, Billie!

SHE'S HERE FOR US

Billie knows what it's like to be a superfan and wants to be the kind of artist who is approachable. *"I consciously have been the artist I would have wanted to have been a fan of growing up,"* she says.

BILLIE ♡ HER FANS

It's a mutual appreciation society

SHE SEES US AS HER FRIENDS

We're all in this together, guys. Billie knows she can't be friends with everyone, but if ever an opportunity arises, she loves hanging out with her fans. *"There's this group of girls I've met a couple times and they're cool as hell. I just was friends with them."* Can we be your friend, Billie?

SHE LOVES FAN GIFTS

If you're thinking of making Billie something, get in line. Billie is used to receiving gifts from fans. She has even received a stuffed blohsh—the human outline Billie uses as a symbol. Cute!

CREDITS

Front cover: PHOTOS: Jason Richardson / Alamy Images, Ivan Kamzyst / Alamy Images.
4–5: PHOTOS: UPI / Alamy Images.
6–7: WORDS: *New York Times*. PHOTOS: Jason Richardson / Alamy Images, UPI / Alamy Images.
8–9: WORDS: NME, Ssense, *Paper* magazine, Coup de Main. PHOTOS: Gonzales Photo /
Alamy Images, ZUMA Press, Inc. / Alamy Images, Andie Mills / Alamy Images.
10–11: WORDS: Billboard, NME, Ssense. PHOTOS: Pacific Press Agency / Alamy Images,
MediaPunch Inc / Alamy Images, WENN Rights Ltd / Alamy Images.
12–13: WORDS: Stereogum.com, Ssense. PHOTOS: ZUMA Press, Inc. / Alamy Images.
14–15: PHOTOS: Roberto Finizio / Alamy Images, Gonzales Photo / Alamy Images.
16–17: WORDS: Luxury Insider, NME. PHOTOS: Gonzales Photo / Alamy Images, WENN Rights Ltd /
Alamy Images, Paul Smith / Alamy Images, Jeffrey Mayer / Alamy Images.
18–19: WORDS: FemaleMag, Bustle, Yahoo. PHOTOS: WENN Rights Ltd / Alamy Images,
ZUMA Press, Inc. / Alamy Images, Image Press Agency / Alamy Images.
20–21: WORDS: *Rolling Stone*. PHOTOS: dpa picture alliance / Alamy Images,
WENN Rights Ltd / Alamy Images, Roberto Finizio / Alamy Images.
22–23: WORDS: Buzzfeed. PHOTOS: MediaPunch Inc / Alamy Images, Image Press Agency /
Alamy Images, Pacific Press Agency / Alamy Images, YouTube / Darkroom/Interscope Records.
24–25: WORDS: MTV News. PHOTOS: Image Press Agency / Alamy Images,
Darkroom/Interscope Records.
26–27: WORDS: *LA Times*, *Seventeen*. PHOTOS: Zoonar GmbH / Alamy Images,
ZUMA Press, Inc. / Alamy Images.
28–29: PHOTOS: Andy Gallagher / Alamy Images, ZUMA Press, Inc. / Alamy Images,
MediaPunch Inc / Alamy Images.
30–31: WORDS: Billboard, Soompi.com, *New York Times*, *Metro*.
PHOTOS: YouTube / Darkroom/Interscope Records.
32–33: WORDS: *Tidal*, *Rolling Stone*, *New York Times*, *The Times*.
PHOTOS: Image Press Agency / Alamy Images, Pacific Press Agency / Alamy Images.
34–35: WORDS: PopBuzz, Coup de Main. PHOTOS: UPI / Alamy Images,
Pacific Press Agency / Alamy Images.
36–37: WORDS: MTV News, *Marie Claire*, *Elle*, BBC. PHOTOS: Pacific Press Agency / Alamy Images.
38–39: PHOTOS: dpa picture alliance / Alamy Images, ZUMA Press, Inc. / Alamy Images,
Darkroom/Interscope Records.
40–41: WORDS: *US Vogue*, NME, Beats1, PopBuzz, NPR. PHOTOS: Pacific Press Agency / Alamy Images.
42–43: WORDS: *Elle*, *Vogue Australia*. PHOTOS: Andie Mills / Alamy Images.
44–45: WORDS: Variance Magazine. PHOTOS: MediaPunch Inc / Alamy Images.
46–47: WORDS: *Elle*, PopSugar. PHOTOS: dpa picture alliance / Alamy Images,
WENN Rights Ltd / Alamy Images, PictureLux / The Hollywood Archive / Alamy Images,
Pacific Press Agency / Alamy Images, Andie Mills / Alamy Images.
48–49: WORDS: NME, Vice, Altpress. PHOTOS: ZUMA Press, Inc. / Alamy Images.
50–51: WORDS: *The Times*, Ad Council. PHOTOS: Guy Bell / Alamy Images,
ZUMA Press, Inc. / Alamy Images, UPI / Alamy Images.
52–53: WORDS: *Elle*, *Harper's Bazaar*, Billboard. PHOTOS: dpa picture alliance / Alamy Images,
Newscom / Alamy Images.
54–55: WORDS: Pigeons and Planes, *New York Times*, *Variety*.
PHOTOS: ZUMA Press, Inc. / Alamy Images, Everett Collection Inc / Alamy Images.
56–57: WORDS: NME, 3voor12, *The Guardian*, *Rolling Stone*. PHOTOS: Image Press Agency /
Alamy Images, dpa picture alliance / Alamy Images, Ivan Kamzyst / Alamy Images.
58–59: WORDS: *Harper's Bazaar*, *Rolling Stone*, *The Guardian*, *Paper* magazine.
PHOTOS: Guy Bell / Alamy Images, dpa picture alliance / Alamy Images, MediaPunch Inc / Alamy Images,
YouTube / Darkroom/Interscope Records.
60–61: WORDS: iHeart Radio, Apple Music. PHOTOS: Gonzales Photo / Alamy Images,
ZUMA Press, Inc. / Alamy Images.
62–63: WORDS: *The Guardian*, *Tidal*, *Variety*, *Rolling Stone*, Vanity Fair. PHOTOS: Gonzales Photo /
Alamy Images, MediaPunch Inc / Alamy Images, Per Grunditz / Alamy Images.
Back cover: PHOTOS: Pacific Press Agency / Alamy Images.